PROJECTING BRITAIN

'Here during a quarter of a century were made many films
projecting Britain and the British character.'

Inscription on Ealing Studios commemorative plaque

PROJECTING BRITAIN

Ealing Studios Film Posters

Edited by David Wilson

With an introduction by Bevis Hillier

BFI PUBLISHING bfi

First published in 1982

by the British Film Institute
127 Charing Cross Road
London WC2H 0EA

Designed by Gillian Crampton Smith

Printed by Merlin Colour Printers
Canvey Island Essex

Copyright © British Film Institute 1982

British Library Cataloguing in Publication data

Projecting Britain: Ealing Studios film posters
1. Ealing Studios
2. Film posters, English
I. Wilson, David
769'.4979143'0942   PN1995.9.P5
ISBN 0 85170 122 1

Acknowledgments

My thanks to S. John Woods, Advertising Director at
Ealing Studios from 1943 to 1955, who commissioned
most of the posters illustrated here and whose help in
the making of this book has been invaluable. Thanks
also to Michelle Snapes, head of the Stills Library at the
British Film Institute, who has helped on this project
from the start; to Elizabeth Heasman, who shepherded
the collection of Ealing posters held in the National
Film Archive; to J.D. Millen for making transparencies
of the posters; and to John Armstrong for biographical
information. Acknowledgment is made to EMI Ltd. for
permission to reproduce the posters of which they hold
the copyright, to MGM for permission to reproduce the
poster for Barnacle Bill, and to Raymond Rohauer for
permission to reproduce the poster for They Came to a
City.

INTRODUCTION

By Bevis Hillier

In 1970, the Duchess of Bedford – 'Nicole Nobody' – staged an exhibition of 'The Architecture of Henry Holland' in the sculpture gallery of Woburn Abbey (which Holland had designed). At the opening, she made a speech. The Duchess was voluble, and spoke the Queen's English – but unfortunately it was Queen Marie Antoinette's. In reporting her in *The Times*, I rather caddishly mimicked her French accent: ''Enry 'Olland was one of the great English architects.'

The Duchess was more amused than offended by this. She telephoned me on the day the report appeared. 'All my friends have rung me up to say, ''Why you not learn to speak English?''' She remembered me from the exhibition private view: we had chatted about Holland's foreman, who had the enjoyable name of Mr Gotobed. 'Why I am really ringing,' the Duchess said, 'is to ask if you can come and stay next weekend.' I accepted. When I arrived, she said: 'We 'ave given you the bedroom with the Gainsborough. I 'ope you like 'im.' It was the first of many weekends I was to spend at Woburn, with guest-lists which included Rex Harrison, Paul Getty, Iris Murdoch, Sir Roy Strong and the Duke's chief rival in the stately home business, the Marquess of Bath.

On this first occasion my fellow guests included John Morley, director of the Royal Pavilion, Brighton, and his wife. At the end of the weekend, the Duke asked his chauffeur to drive us down to London. We sat in the back of the huge chestnut-brown Bentley (number-plate DOB 2) driven by the brown-uniformed chauffeur. It seemed as high as a double-decker bus: we peered down on the roofs of Minis that overtook us as we made our stately progress down the M.1. As the limousine purred along, John Morley, who was in the front seat next to the chauffeur, turned to me and said, 'It's all a bit Ealing Comedy, isn't it?'

I knew just what he meant. As in an Ealing film, we had a brief taste of fantasy; we were living the life the English are expected to live, not the life they do live. In Ealing films, as in Agatha Christie novels, colonels are always *crusty old* colonels; spinsters are *prim* and *ramrod-backed*. Servants say things like 'Very pleased, I'm sure'. The rich are always *stinking* rich. There is an irony in this, when one remembers that most of the Ealing films were made on a shoestring budget, with actors who were often living on short commons. The Ealing films helped perpetuate an image of the English which had either never existed at all, or had been shattered for ever by the First World War. We have never lived it down. It was not counteracted by Swinging London of the 1960s, or incinerated in the white heat of the technological revolution. It is the image that foreigners like to preserve of us: a country deeply but entertainingly divided by class; full of eccentrics, stiff-upper-lipped and doggedly clinging to a picturesque archaism. It has probably done our international standing permanent harm and helped to intensify class warfare at home.

To a country which fondly imagined in the 1960s that it had achieved 'the classless society', the image of the

English preserved in Ealing films may seem hopelessly naive – as naive as the novelist who tells us of one of his characters that 'he went black with anger'. Nobody ever went black with anger, and even the English aristocracy was never quite as dotty as that portrayed in *Kind Hearts and Coronets*. But in mitigation it must be pointed out that the movie industry as a whole was still (compared with painting and literature) in its infancy – and perhaps it still is. A few silent films, which must rank among movie *incunabula,* had shown what majestic art could result when the medium was properly exploited; but in Hollywood the integrity of the medium was constantly sabotaged by the overriding demand for box-office success. *Gone with the Wind* now seems an overblown and endlessly vapid extravaganza. Like *nouveau-riche* people, Hollywood movie-makers wanted to make it clear that they had millions to spend. So they made florid, show-off movies, bursting with meretricious splendours. Ealing Studios did not have the millions. Their naiveté was of a more suburban kind. The films belonged to the same period and genre as Wilfred Pickles' popular radio show 'Have a Go', whose signature tunes were 'Have a Go, Joe' and 'Come round, any old time, make yerself at home; Put yer feet on the mantelpiece . . .' That kind of cosiness was endemic in Ealing films. Not just in the comedies; even films like *The Cruel Sea*, which were meant to convey some kind of epic quality, were cosily reassuring, gave a warm inner glow like Bovril. *The Cruel Sea* confirmed Britons' agreeable consciousness that they were better than anyone else, ruled the waves, and never never never would be slaves.

One thing that was not naive about the films was the posters for them – for here the art in question was not the new unpractised art of film-making, but the ancient arts of draughtsmanship and design. The art of the poster was in its high maturity, almost its swansong period (for mainly graphic posters gave way after the 1950s to mainly photographic ones). And the artists who designed the posters were not cutting their teeth on a new discipline and learning by trial and error as they proceeded. Most of them had had a gruelling training, on classic principles, in art schools; and many of them had considerable reputations beyond their poster work – they were 'canvas' artists first, commercial artists second.

I do not mean to sneer at Ealing films, or to make the 'simplistic' suggestion that the films were bad, the posters good. (Though the film critic C.A. Lejeune was almost prepared to go that far in the *Observer* of 17 May 1953 when writing of a non-Ealing film: 'The most interesting contribution to the week's cinema has been not a picture but a picture about a picture: Ronald Searle's delightful poster for *The Oracle.*') But I would think it fair to suggest that the Ealing posters have a higher place in the canon of world poster art (certainly that of *film* poster art) than Ealing films occupy in movie history.

Much of the credit for the quality of Ealing film posters must go to S. John Woods, who had been employed by Fox Films in the 1930s and was appointed to the Ealing Studios advertising department in 1943 to implement the enlightened advertising policy which had been initiated by Monja Danischewsky. He worked directly under Michael Balcon, the head of production, from 1947 until Ealing closed in 1959. Woods was no slouch as a designer himself, as several of the posters in this book show. Born in 1915, he was trained as a graphic designer and painter and also became an art critic. In the 1930s he exhibited abstract paintings and promoted abstract art in articles and in the exhibitions he organised. He also designed posters for the Old Vic, Covent Garden and Sadlers Wells. But his years at Ealing proved that his greatest skill was as an impresario, marshalling and encouraging and exploiting to best advantage the talents of other artists. He was to Ealing Films what Jack Beddington was to Shell and Frank Pick to London Transport.

Woods recruited an impressive 'stable' of artists, including John Piper, Edward Bawden, James Fitton, John Minton, Mervyn Peake, Edward Ardizzone, Leslie Hurry, Ronald Searle, Barnett Freedman, James Boswell and Reginald Mount. I asked Mr Woods how far he gave directions to the artists, and how far he left them to their own devices. 'I decided which artists to commission both in relation to their work and in relation to what I thought was the feeling of the film. Some of the artists, such as Bawden, were experienced in lettering. But some of them were purely painters, and with them I worked closely on the lettering. Apart from that, I wanted the artists to give their own interpretation of the subject.' Several of the posters are designed with a collage technique: a photographic still of one or more of the film's stars is superimposed on graphic work. A good example is John Piper's design for *Pink String and Sealing Wax* (1945) with a still of Googie Withers in front of Piper's drawing of a Regency Brighton terrace. I asked Mr Woods whether it was his policy to introduce a fragment of the film's reality into otherwise graphic designs. 'Oh, no. There would certainly have been no question of superimposing a photographic image on a drawing submitted by John Piper: that must have been part of his design.'

James Fitton RA designed the poster for what many people regard as Ealing Studios' best film, *Kind Hearts and Coronets* (in which Dennis Price murders his way towards a dukedom through eight victims, all played by Alec Guinness). Fitton was born in the reign of Queen Victoria, in which the film is set, and was already fifty in 1949 when he designed the poster. He had worked for Frank Pick, who had talent-spotted him at a Leicester Galleries exhibition. For Pick he had designed posters of a tightrope bicyclist at the Holborn Empire and of ballet dancers at Sadlers Wells, later adding the respective legends, in attractive ribbon lettering, 'Variety for a change' and 'Just a step by Underground'. S. John Woods had seen these designs and thought Fitton had the lightness of touch to represent on posters *Kind Hearts and Coronets* whose director, Robert Hamer, was warned by Michael Balcon: 'You are trying to sell that most unsaleable commodity to the British – irony.' Just before he died James Fitton told me: 'I went down to the studios at Ealing and made sketches. I also had lunch in a pub with Alec Guinness and some of the other actors, and made more sketches.' The poster showed Valerie Hobson and Joan Greenwood in elaborate veiled and decorated hats, with Dennis Price clutching the bars of a jail cell in the background. Already in this poster there is evidence of the whimsicality which replaced the 'Britain Can Take It' earnestness of the wartime and immediate post-war periods.

In a book of 1975, *Austerity/Binge: Decorative Arts of the Forties and Fifties*, I suggested that the Festival of Britain (1951) divided the grim 1940s (Austerity) from the ebullient 1950s ('Binge'), rather as the Depression of 1929 was a caesura between the frivolous 1920s and the serious 1930s. And I tried to isolate and analyse the distinctive characteristics of both decades – the decades in which the best Ealing posters were designed. My book began with 'The Arts of War' – 'When you are waging a war, you have other things to think of than decoration.' Ealing Studios 'did their bit' for the war effort – and more – in sixteen wartime films about the war: *Let George Do It* (1940), *Convoy* (1940), *Sailors Three* (1940), *Spare a Copper* (1940), *Ships with Wings* (1941), *The Big Blockade* (1942), *The Foreman went to France* (1942), *Next of Kin* (1942), *The Goose Steps Out* (1942), *Nine Men* (1943), *The Bells Go Down* (1943), *Undercover* (1943), *Went the Day Well?* (1943), *San Demetrio London* (1943), *For Those in Peril* (1944), and *Johnny Frenchman* (1945). The war ended before *Johnny Frenchman* was released, and after it Ealing wisely produced few war films. These included *The Captive Heart* (1946) about prisoner-of-war life in Germany, *The Overlanders* (1946) about the evacuation of a herd of cattle from an area threatened by Japanese attack, and *Against the Wind* (1948) – saboteurs at work against the Nazis in wartime Belgium. *Against the Wind* was a box-office disaster, and Ealing got the message. There were to be no more wartime dramas until *The Cruel Sea* (1953) and *Dunkirk* (1958), and these two were not war-nostalgia movies, glorifying warfare, but rueful evocations of hardship and (in the case of *Dunkirk*) defeat.

After the war, the combatant nations retreated into their shells. The British became aggressively British – something very evident in the Ealing films. 'It was Balcon's mission,' George Perry writes, 'to present the British character, or his idea of it. He regarded the British as individualists who were not averse to joining up with each other to battle against a common cause. He saw a nation tolerant of harmless eccentricities, but determinedly opposed to anti-social behaviour.'[*] It was the Britishness of Ealing films which prevented most of

---

[*]George Perry, *Forever Ealing* (Pavilion, London, 1981)

them from having box-office success in America or their actors from becoming stars there. One Ealing actress, Gracie Fields, was taken up by Hollywood, but Alec Guinness waited years to achieve Hollywood acclaim, and Googie Withers and Diana Dors (who might have been a natural successor to Mae West) were never big names in America. The pathological insularity of the British in the later 1940s is symbolically satirised in *Passport to Pimlico* (1949) in which the inhabitants of a London district find they are legally Burgundians and palisade themselves off from post-war rationing and restrictions, and in its immediate successor *Whisky Galore!*, which is actually about an island ('Todday' – in real life Eriskay) and the determination of the islanders to stop mainland bureaucrats doing them out of a cargo of whisky which arrives on their shore through shipwreck.

The nationalistic, insular feeling had a strong effect on the decorative arts. In *Austerity/Binge* I wrote:

The British and Americans looked to their own traditional cultures for inspiration. The ornament, gaiety and pattern for which Geoffrey Boumphrey felt a need, they found in the bright bold motifs of folk art. In England this meant in particular adopting designs from the circus, the fairground, gypsy caravans and painted narrow-boats (improperly called 'barges') of the English canals. Men who had been away from their own land for years, men who were sick of the Continent and its embroilments, rediscovered their own country with a kind of infatuation.

The folk art of the English music-hall had already been celebrated in *Champagne Charlie* (1944), in which Tommy Trinder and Stanley Holloway re-enacted the rivalries of the singers George Leybourne and the Great Vance in the 1860s. In the striking poster for this film, S. John Woods made use of the harlequin fairground lettering which was to be so popular in Ealing posters of the 1950s, including *The Ladykillers* (1955). *Champagne Charlie* showed the characteristic 1940s nostalgia for the Victorian period, the time before the old England and its values had been disrupted by two world wars: *Pink String and Sealing Wax* (1945) was a Victorian melodrama; *Nicholas Nickleby* (1947), with posters by Edward Ardizzone, was released at the same time as

David Lean's *Great Expectations; The Loves of Joanna Godden* (1947) was an Edwardian drama set on Romney Marsh; and *Kind Hearts and Coronets* (1949) was also set in the Edwardian age.

The folk art of the narrow-boats was celebrated in *Painted Boats* (1945) and its beautifully designed poster by John Piper, into which another kind of British folk art was introduced, for the elaborate cartouche around the lettering was from a rubbing Piper had made from a slate tomb in Leicestershire or Nottinghamshire. Piper had come to know S. John Woods because, before Piper met his wife Myfanwy (heroine of two John Betjeman poems), Woods and Myfanwy had both played hockey in a scratch team organised by Professor C.E.M. Joad of 'Brains Trust' fame. Piper also knew Michael Balcon through the English Opera Group in which he was involved with Benjamin Britten and Peter Pears: there was some talk of Balcon's filming operas, and although nothing came of that, he gave the Group money. Piper's first Ealing poster was for *The Bells Go Down* (1943), a Tommy Trinder film set in the London blitz.

Piper confirms that it was he who combined the still of Googie Withers and the drawing of Brighton in his poster for *Pink String and Sealing Wax*. 'I had been working in Brighton on a book for Duckworth called *Brighton Aquatints*. In the limited edition of fifty, all fifty copies of one aquatint, ''Brighton from the Station Yard'', were hand-coloured by John Betjeman. He used to come down to Henley every evening on the 5.15 – at the time he was working for Sidney Bernstein in the Films Division of the Ministry of Information. ''I haven't done my aquatint,'' he would say. ''I must get it done before dinner''.'

Another aspect of the 1940s decorative arts to which I drew attention in *Austerity/Binge* was the taste for the occult, Gothick fantasy and ghost stories. 'Ruins, follies and ghosts were part of the happy old England, and part of the stock-in-trade of the new romantic movement in painting led by John Piper and Graham Sutherland.' Piper had designed a fine Gothick jacket for the first edition of Henry Green's novel *Loving* (1945). He also designed Gothick Strawberry Hill settings for Frederick Ashton's ballet 'The Quest' (1943). The ballet 'The Haunted Ballroom' was revived at Sadlers Wells in 1945. G.W. Stonier's *The Memoirs of a Ghost*, with an appropriate jacket design by Eva Haman, appeared in 1949. John Farleigh illustrated *Haunted England* (1940) with spooky pen-and-ink drawings. The British film industry was not left behind in this chase after will-o'-the-wisps. A film adaptation of Sheridan Le Fanu's *Uncle Silas*, with Derrick de Marney in the sinister title role and Jean Simmons as Caroline Ruthyn, was screened in 1947. Ealing's first venture into the supernatural (if one excepts *The Ghost of St. Michael's*, a Will Hay farce of 1941) was *Halfway House* (1944), about a group of travellers staying at an inn that had been bombed a year earlier. The poster, showing the guests in the foreground, the eerie inn in the background, was by Matvyn Wright, described by S. John Woods as 'a good artist who completely gave up art – and anybody connected with it – about the late 1950s'. Leslie Hurry designed a nightmarish poster of coffins, skeletons and bats for the ghost-story film *Dead of Night* (1945). Hurry, who had been 'discovered' by the ballet dancer Robert Helpmann at an exhibition of his work, had made his name with an ominous set for the ballet of *Hamlet* (1942), a composition dominated by a vengeful, dagger-brandishing figure. Leslie Hurry died in 1978, leaving many of his designs and posters, including that for *Dead of Night*, to his nephew John Armstrong, himself a talented film-maker. A late Ealing venture into the occult was made in 1955 with *The Night My Number Came Up*, about a dream that predicts an aeroplane crash. What explains the 1940s preoccupation with ghosts? Perhaps it had something to do with the numbers of men so recently killed. More probably it was part of the general escapism from a depressed and austere period, the post-war convalescence.

Another form of escape was into surrealism. There is a touch of surrealism in the poster for *The Captive Heart* (1946), the prisoner-of-war film – a heart with wings behind a grid of barbed wire. There is a surreal air reminiscent of de Chirico's paintings in H.A. Rothholz's poster for the film of J.B. Priestley's *They Came to a City* (1944), which was after all a film with a surreal plot about a group of people arriving at the gates of Utopia. This design incorporated the exaggerated 'vanishing point' perspective familiar in surrealist paintings, a design cliché which recurs in the posters for *The Ghost of St. Michael's* (1941), *Behind These Walls* (a 1947 poster by S. John Woods for an Anglo-French film), *Train of Events* (1949, Reginald Mount), *Passport to Pimlico* (1949, S. John Woods) and *The Magnet* (1950 – not Ardizzone's design but Simmons' more dramatic bombscape).

By 1951, with the bright, optimistic Festival of Britain, the post-war convalescence was ending. Note that the origin of the Festival was again a harking back to Victorian England – marking the centenary of the Great Exhibition of 1851. But note also that this was not an international exhibition, as in 1851, at which the nations of the world would pit their excellences against each other: it was a Festival of *Britain*. From here the 1950s would gather momentum to the point in 1957 when Harold Macmillan was alleged to have said 'You've never had it so good'. A mood of devil-may-care frivolity had set in soon after the First World War. The 1940s austerity kept it at bay longer after the Second World War, but in the 1950s a kind of national flightiness supervened. It was already visible at the Festival, in the whimsy of Emett's fanciful railway. The 1950s love of archaic Victorian and Edwardian transport – balloons in *Around the World in Eighty Days*, old crock cars in *Genevieve*, penny-farthing bicycles as a wallpaper motif – was evident in the 1953 Ealing comedy *The Titfield Thunderbolt*, about villagers fighting a branch line closure by taking over the railway themselves and stealing a Victorian locomotive from the Science Museum. Edward Bawden designed an appropriately whimsical poster, in which the names of the actors appear in the steam coming from the locomotive's tall funnel. Bawden was a veteran of poster work. He had designed several posters for the London Underground. His first commission for Ealing had been his delightfully Edward Learish poster for *Hue and Cry* (1947). He recalls that he made about six visits to the Studios and talked mainly with 'a man with a Russian name' (i.e. Monja Danischewsky, who called his 1966 autobiography *White Russian, Red Face*). 'I was given a completely free hand,' Bawden recalls. 'Perhaps I ought to have been given more guidance. I worked completely

THE POSTERS

1944   For Those in Peril

Directed by Charles Crichton, script by Harry Watt, J.O.C. Orton, T.E.B.
Clarke from a story by Richard Hillary. With David Farrar, Ralph Michael,
Robert Wyndham, John Slater.
Documentary-style drama about the wartime air-sea rescue service, Charles
Crichton's debut as a director. The story was by Richard Hillary, the fighter
pilot who wrote *The Last Enemy* and was later killed in action.

1944   Champagne Charlie

Directed by Alberto Cavalcanti, script by Austin Melford, Angus Macphail, John Dighton. With Tommy Trinder, Stanley Holloway, Jean Kent, Betty Warren.
Trinder and Holloway as rival performers in the music halls of mid-Victorian England.
S. John Woods' poster design incorporated drawings by Eric Fraser; the title was designed by Barnett Freedman.

Among the films distributed by Ealing were some of the thrillers in the Charlie Chan series produced by the American company Monogram. The films were directed by Phil Rosen from scripts by George Callahan, with Sidney Toler as the Chinese detective and Mantan Moreland as his black chauffeur. S. John Woods designed, or commissioned, posters for the British release.

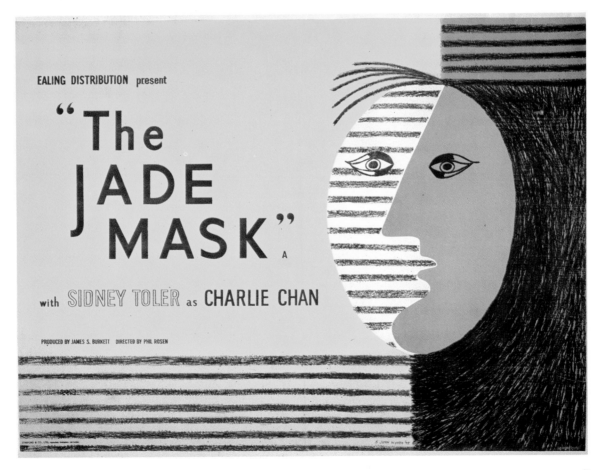

1947   Frieda

Directed by Basil Dearden, script by Angus Macphail, Ronald Millar from the
play by Ronald Millar. With Mai Zetterling, David Farrar, Glynis Johns, Flora
Robson, Albert Lieven.
An RAF officer brings home his German wife during the last months of the
war. Mai Zetterling's British debut.

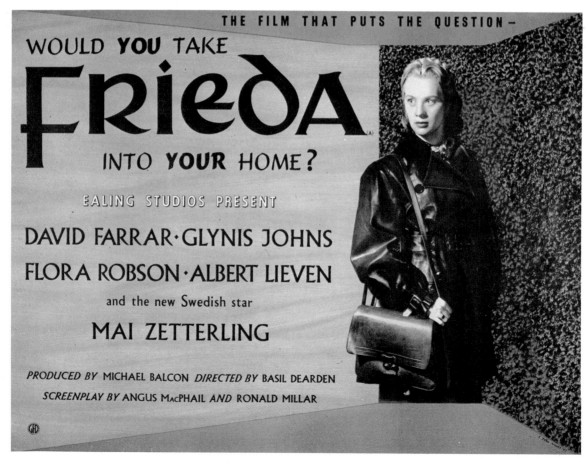

Directed by Henry Cornelius, script by T.E.B. Clarke. With Stanley Holloway, Betty Warren, Raymond Huntley, Barbara Murray, Paul Dupuis, Margaret Rutherford, Basil Radford, Naunton Wayne.
The people of the London district of Pimlico discover that, according to ancient charter, they are actually Burgundians and declare their independence from the United Kingdom. The first of a trio of successful comedies released by the studio in 1949.
The drawing on the poster is by the cartoonist Nicolas Bentley.

1950   Cage of Gold

Directed by Basil Dearden, script by Jack Whittingham from a story by Jack
Whittingham and Paul Stein. With Jean Simmons, David Farrar, James
Donald, Herbert Lom.
Melodrama with Jean Simmons as an artist menaced by the lover who has
abandoned her.

1951   The Lavender Hill Mob

Directed by Charles Crichton, script by T.E.B. Clarke. With Alec Guinness, Stanley Holloway, Sidney James, Alfie Bass.

A mild-mannered bank clerk masterminds a bullion robbery and the export of the gold as souvenir models of the Eiffel Tower. The Bank of England itself provided the robbery plan. T.E.B. Clarke's script, which includes a parody of *The Blue Lamp* police car chase, won an Oscar.

Ronald Searle's subsequent work included the 'St. Trinian's' series.

1951   The Man in the White Suit

Directed by Alexander Mackendrick, script by Roger Macdougall, Alexander
Mackendrick, John Dighton from a play by Roger Macdougall. With Alec
Guinness, Joan Greenwood, Cecil Parker, Michael Gough, Ernest Thesiger.
A laboratory assistant in a textile mill discovers an everlasting fibre but is
thwarted by management and unions alike.

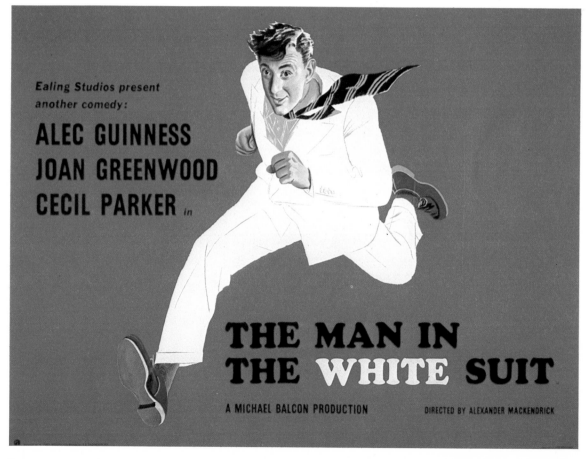

Directed by John Harlow. With David Farrar, Anne Crawford, John Stuart. A reporter investigating a murder discovers that his news editor is compromised. A crime thriller produced at Ealing, though not strictly an Ealing production.

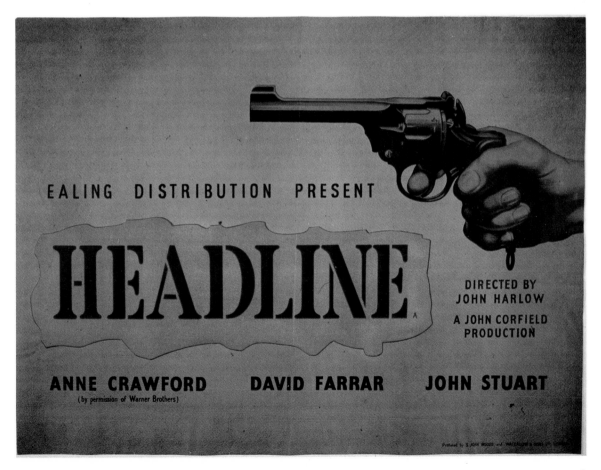

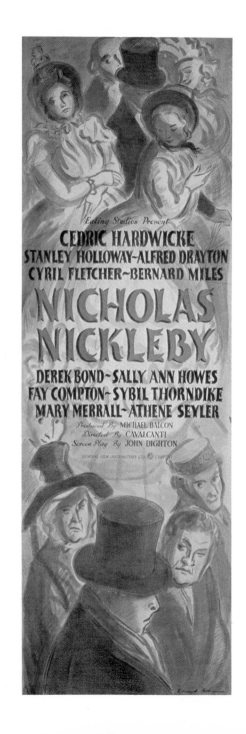

1947   Nicholas Nickleby

Directed by Alberto Cavalcanti, script by John Dighton from the novel by
Charles Dickens. With Derek Bond, Cedric Hardwicke, Mary Merrall, Sally
Ann Howes, Bernard Miles, Sybil Thorndike, Stanley Holloway.
Cavalcanti's adaptation of Dickens' novel was his last Ealing production.
Released a year after David Lean's *Great Expectations*, the Ealing Dickens drew
unfavourable comparisons.

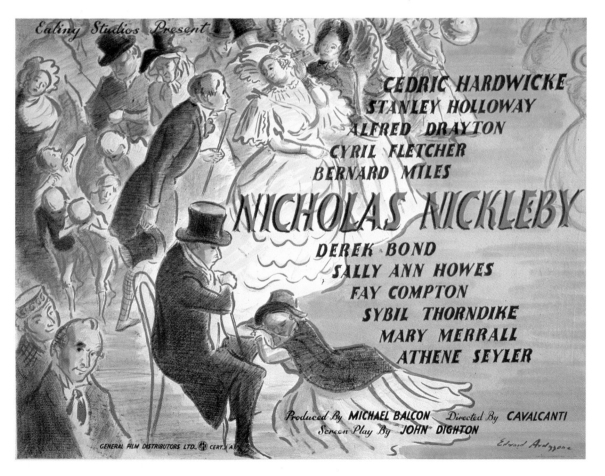

1950   The Magnet

Directed by Charles Frend, script by T.E.B. Clarke. With Stephen Murray, William Fox, Kay Walsh, Meredith Edwards.

A comedy about a psychiatrist's son whose magnet involves him in a series of adventures. The child was played by William Fox, later James Fox of *The Servant*. James Robertson Justice masqueraded as Seamas Mor na Feasag to play a tramp.

'And this is true not only of us here in our little wire-enclosed cinder patch, but also of the scores of other camps, great sprawling towns of twenty thousand men, or hamlets of a few hundred: each a little piece of England.'

From the script of The Captive Heart

1946   The Captive Heart

Directed by Basil Dearden, script by Angus Macphail, Guy Morgan from a story by Patrick Kirwan. With Michael Redgrave, Jack Warner, Rachel Kempson, Mervyn Johns, Basil Radford, Gladys Henson, Jimmy Hanley. British POWs, and the women who wait for their release. The main story features Michael Redgrave as a Czech who assumes the identity of a dead British officer. The film was partly shot in the British occupation zone of Germany.

1947 Hue and Cry

Directed by Charles Crichton, script by T.E.B. Clarke. With Alastair Sim, Jack Warner, Harry Fowler, Valerie White.

London boys outwit a gang of crooks. The first of T.E.B. Clarke's Ealing comedies. The celebrated climax has hundreds of boys converging on a bombsite to trap the crooks.

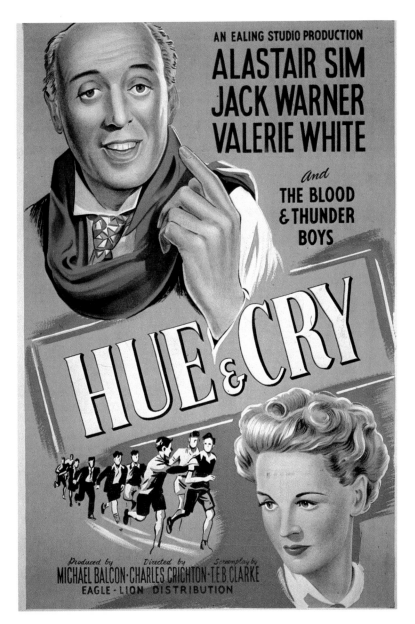

1953   The Titfield Thunderbolt

Directed by Charles Crichton, script by T.E.B. Clarke. With Stanley Holloway, John Gregson, George Relph, Naunton Wayne, Godfrey Tearle.
A village community defends its local railway, threatened with closure by the authorities. The West Country branch line used in the filming was itself later closed.

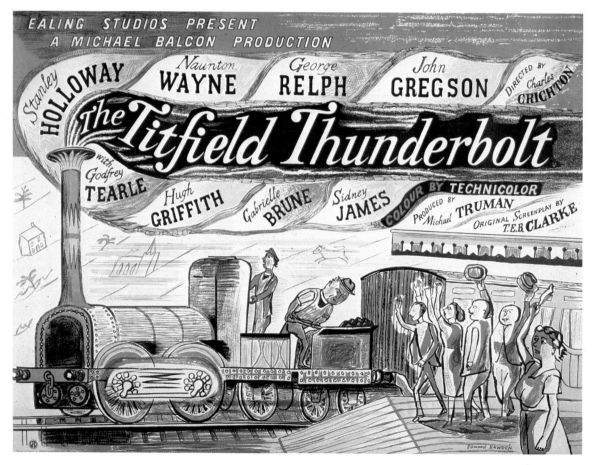

1947 It Always Rains on Sunday

Directed by Robert Hamer, script by Angus Macphail, Robert Hamer, Henry Cornelius from the novel by Arthur la Bern. With Googie Withers, Edward Chapman, Susan Shaw, John McCallum, Jack Warner, Patricia Plunkett.
An East End housewife shelters a former lover on the run from the police. A gallery of character actors provided the local colour.

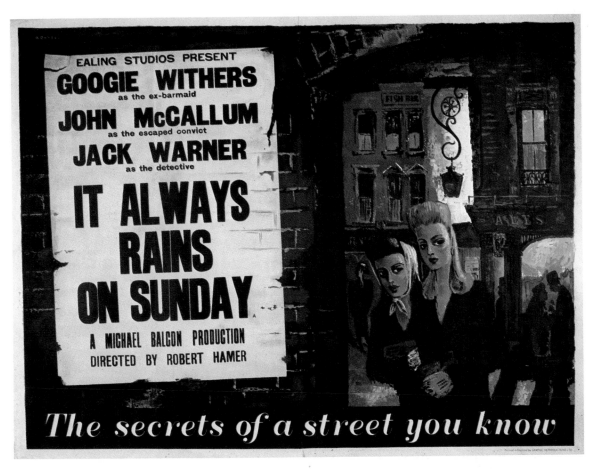

1950   The Blue Lamp

Directed by Basil Déarden, script by T.E.B. Clarke from a story by Ted Willis, Jan Read. With Jack Warner, Jimmy Hanley, Dirk Bogarde, Robert Flemyng, Peggy Evans.

Ealing's tribute to the Metropolitan Police, under pressure from the post-war crime wave and a new breed of criminal. Jack Warner's P.C. Dixon was resurrected for the subsequent long-running television series *Dixon of Dock Green*. Alexander Mackendrick directed the car chase on location in the streets of West London.

1949   Kind Hearts and Coronets

Directed by Robert Hamer, script by Robert Hamer, John Dighton from the novel *Israel Rank* by Roy Horniman. With Dennis Price, Alec Guinness, Joan Greenwood, Valerie Hobson.

Ealing's most celebrated film, a black comedy in which Dennis Price murders his way to a dukedom, with Alec Guinness as his multiple victims. Michael Balcon told Hamer: 'You are trying to sell the most unsaleable commodity to the British – irony. Good luck to you.' Hamer commented that he wanted to make a film 'which paid no regard whatever to established, though not practised, moral convention'.

1945   Johnny Frenchman

Directed by Charles Frend, script by T.E.B. Clarke. With Françoise Rosay,
Tom Walls, Patricia Roc, Ralph Michael, Paul Dupuis.
The Cornish and Breton fishing communities, rivals before the war, are
united by a common cause. Ealing's last wartime film, hastily updated when
peace was declared. A Cornish village was dressed up as Brittany.

1946   The Overlanders

Directed by Harry Watt, script by Harry Watt. With Chips Rafferty, John Nugent Hayward, Daphne Campbell, Jean Blue.
A cattle herd is driven across the Australian outback, out of reach of Japanese air attack. Watt was sent to Australia to make a film about the country's role in the war. The film's success persuaded Ealing to take a lease on studios in Sydney, and over the years a number of Ealing films were made there.

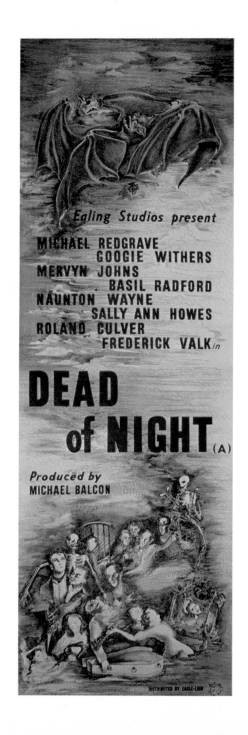

1945   Dead of Night

Directed by Alberto Cavalcanti, Charles Crichton, Basil Dearden, Robert Hamer, script by John V. Baines, Angus Macphail, with additional dialogue by T.E.B. Clarke, from stories by Angus Macphail, E.F. Benson, John V. Baines, H.G. Wells. With Mervyn Johns, Sally Ann Howes, Michael Allan, Googie Withers, Ralph Michael, Basil Radford, Naunton Wayne, Michael Redgrave.

A portmanteau film about the supernatural, five stories linked by a dream. The most celebrated episode, directed by Cavalcanti, features Michael Redgrave as a ventriloquist whose dummy comes 'alive'.

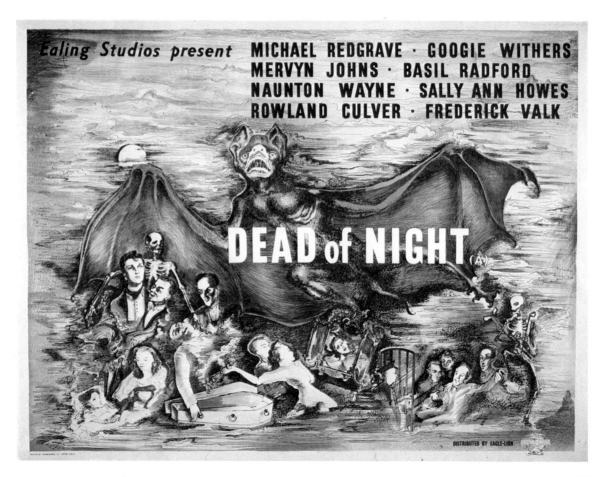

1943 San Demetrio London

Directed by Charles Frend, script by Robert Hamer, Charles Frend from the narrative by F. Tennyson Jesse. With Walter Fitzgerald, Ralph Michael, Frederick Piper, Gordon Jackson, Robert Beatty.
The crew of an abandoned oil tanker reboard the ship and bring her back to port. The film was based on the official record of an actual incident.

'. . . dramas with a documentary background and comedies about ordinary people with the stray eccentric among them — films about day-dreamers, mild anarchists, little men who long to kick the boss in the teeth.'

Michael Balcon

1940   Let George Do It

Directed by Marcel Varnel, script by John Dighton, Austin Melford, Angus Macphail, Basil Dearden. With George Formby, Phyllis Calvert, Garry Marsh, Coral Browne.

George Formby as a pier entertainer accidentally shipped to Norway where he is mistaken for a British agent. The first Ealing film to take the war as its subject, notable for a dream sequence in which Formby descends on a Nazi rally and uses Hitler as a punchbag.

1948   Saraband for Dead Lovers

Directed by Basil Dearden, script by John Dighton, Alexander Mackendrick from the novel by Helen Simpson. With Stewart Granger, Joan Greenwood, Flora Robson, Françoise Rosay, Peter Bull.
The doomed romance between Sophie Dorothea, wife of the Hanoverian Prince who was later to be George I of England, and a soldier Count.
Ealing's first film in colour, a prestige production urged on the studio by J. Arthur Rank. In the event it was a commercial failure.

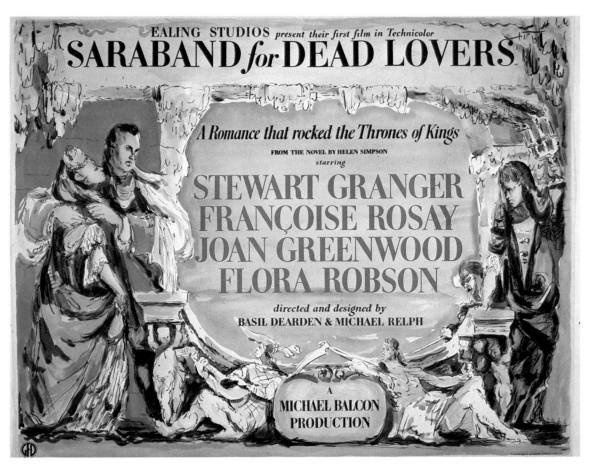

Directed by Ralph Smart, script by W.P. Lipscomb, Monja Danischewsky from a story by Ralph Smart. With Chips Rafferty, Tommy Trinder, Gordon Jackson, Jean Blue, Charles Tingwell.

White settlers clash with an aborigine tribe over land rights. Ealing's third Australian film, and the last to be made at the studio leased in Sydney. The music was by Vaughan Williams.

1947   The Loves of Joanna Godden

Directed by Charles Frend, script by H.E. Bates and Angus Macphail from the novel *Joanna Godden* by Sheila Kaye-Smith. With Googie Withers, John McCallum, Jean Kent, Derek Bond, Chips Rafferty.
Googie Withers inherits a farm in turn-of-the-century Kent and resolves to run it herself. Much of the film was shot on location on Romney Marsh; some scenes were directed by Robert Hamer when Charles Frend fell ill. The music was by Vaughan Williams.

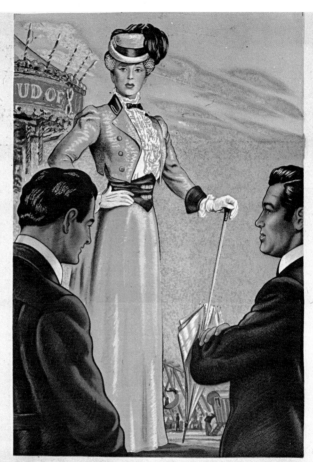

1949   Eureka Stockade

Directed by Harry Watt, script by Harry Watt, Walter Greenwood. With Chips Rafferty, Jane Barrett, Jack Lambert, Gordon Jackson.
Ealing's second Australian film, about the clash between miners and the colonial government following the gold rush of 1853.

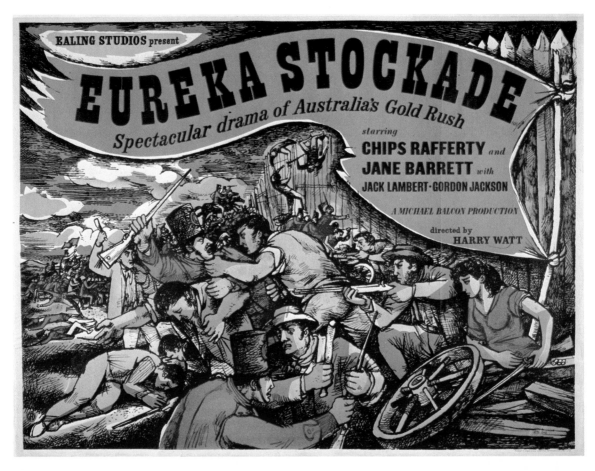

Directed by Harry Watt, script by W.P. Lipscomb, Ralph Smart, Leslie Norman from a story by Harry Watt. With Anthony Steel, Dinah Sheridan, Harold Warrender.
A game-warden in Kenya sets up a national park. A plea for wildlife preservation, and a big box-office success for Ealing.

1949 Train of Events

Directed by Sidney Cole, Charles Crichton, Basil Dearden, script by Basil Dearden, T.E.B. Clarke, Ronald Millar, Angus Macphail. With Jack Warner, Susan Shaw, Joan Dowling, Valerie Hobson, John Clements, Irina Baronova, Peter Finch.

A portmanteau film reconstructing the stories of four people on a night express which crashes. Jack Warner was the engine driver.

1955 The Ladykillers

Directed by Alexander Mackendrick, script by William Rose. With Alec Guinness, Katie Johnson, Peter Sellers, Herbert Lom, Cecil Parker, Danny Green, Jack Warner.

Bank thieves take lodging in the house of a genteel old lady, and come, individually, to a nasty end. Alexander Mackendrick's last film for Ealing and one of the studio's most successful comedies. An archetypically English film scripted by an American and directed by a Scot born in Boston.

1948   Another Shore

Directed by Charles Crichton, script by Walter Meade from the novel by
Kenneth Reddin. With Robert Beatty, Moira Lister, Stanley Holloway.
A Dublin-based comedy, with Robert Beatty as a dreamy Irishman whose
fantasy of life in the South Seas is deflected into the reality of marriage and a
steady job.

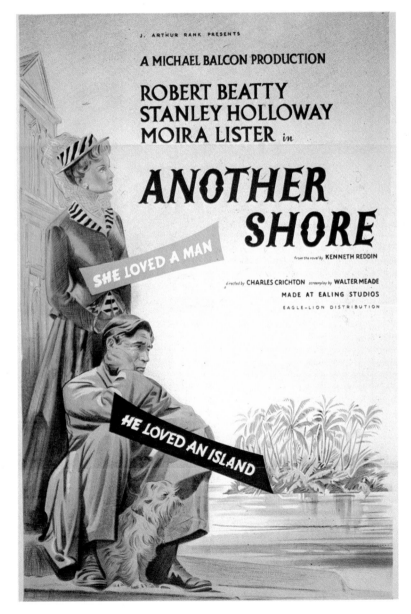

1953 The Cruel Sea

Directed by Charles Frend, script by Eric Ambler from the novel by Nicholas Monsarrat. With Jack Hawkins, Donald Sinden, Denholm Elliott, Virginia McKenna.
A British corvette, captained by Jack Hawkins, hunts U-boats in the Atlantic.
One of Ealing's commercially most successful films.

Alternative poster for The Cruel Sea

'Tucked away in a small street near Marble Arch, under the direction of S. John Woods, himself an artist, this enterprising unit was responsible for a series of the best [film] posters ever devised . . . The designer chosen in each case was the one who seemed best to understand the subject.'

C. A. Lejeune

1944   Black Magic

Another of the films in the Charlie Chan series distributed by Ealing. Directed by Phil Rosen, with Sidney Toler and Mantan Moreland.

1945   Pink String and Sealing Wax

Directed by Robert Hamer, script by Diana Morgan, Robert Hamer from the play by Roland Pertwee. With Mervyn Johns, Googie Withers, Gordon Jackson, Sally Ann Howes.

Late Victorian melodrama, set in Brighton and featuring thwarted romance and murder by poison. Robert Hamer's first full-length film for Ealing.

Directed by Charles Crichton, script by Stephen Black, Micky McCarthy, commentary by Louis MacNeice. With Jenny Laird, Bill Blewitt, May Hallatt, Robert Griffith.

A documentary-style story about life on the English canals. The commentary was spoken by James McKechnie.

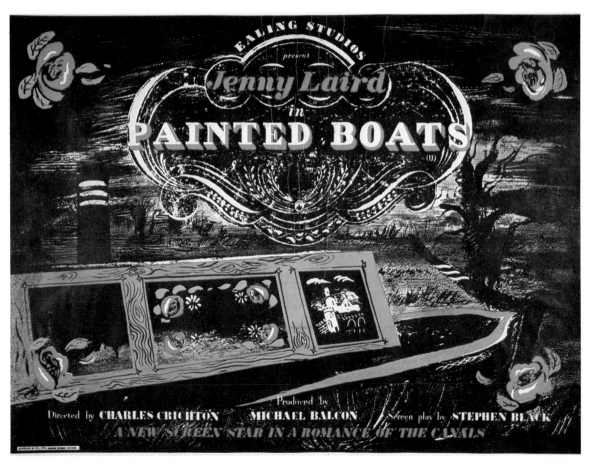

1954 The Love Lottery

Directed by Charles Crichton, script by Harry Kurnitz from a story by Charles
Neilson-Terry, Zelma Bramley Moore, with additional dialogue by Monja
Danischewsky. With David Niven, Peggy Cummins, Anne Vernon, Gordon
Jackson, Herbert Lom.
A film star (David Niven) is first prize in a lottery. Humphrey Bogart appears
in a walk-on part.

1944   The Return of the Vikings

Directed by Charles Frend, script by Sidney Cole and Charles Frend.
A documentary drama about the skipper of a Norwegian whaler who trains as
a paratrooper after the German invasion of Norway. Commissioned by the
Norwegian government in exile.

1944   They Came to a City

Directed by Basil Dearden, script by Basil Dearden, Sidney Cole from the play by J.B. Priestley. With John Clements, Googie Withers, Raymond Huntley, Renée Gadd, A.E. Matthews.

J.B. Priestley's stage play about a group of people, representing a range of class and opinion, who assemble at the gates of a Utopian city and debate whether they should enter the city. The West End stage cast repeated their roles for the film. Priestley himself appeared in a prologue and epilogue.

1945   The Chinese Cat

One of the Charlie Chan series distributed by Ealing. Directed by Phil Rosen, with Sidney Toler and Mantan Moreland.

Directed by John Baxter, script by Reginald Purdell, Bud Flanagan. With Bud Flanagan, Chesney Allen, Teddy Brown, Alfredo Campoli.

Bud Flanagan is concussed and has a series of dreams while awaiting treatment in hospital. The first of two Flanagan and Allen comedies made at Ealing by producer/director John Baxter.

1954   West of Zanzibar

Directed by Harry Watt, script by Jack Whittingham, Max Catto from a story by Harry Watt. With Anthony Steel, Sheila Sim, William Simons, Orlando Martins.

A sequel to *Where No Vultures Fly*. Members of a tribe resettled near Mombasa get involved in ivory smuggling, but a game-warden intervenes on their behalf. Sheila Sim took over from Dinah Sheridan as the warden's wife. The film was banned in Kenya for its paternalist attitude towards the Africans.

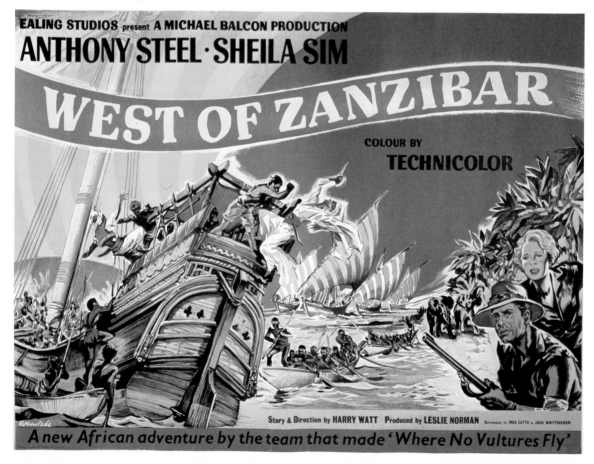

1944   The Halfway House

Directed by Basil Dearden, script by Angus Macphail, Diana Morgan, T.E.B. Clarke from the play *The Peaceful Inn* by Denis Ogden. With Mervyn Johns, Glynis Johns, Tom Walls, Françoise Rosay, Esmond Knight, Guy Middleton, Valerie White, Sally Ann Howes.

A group of travellers arrive at a hotel and find their lives changed by the ghostly proprietor and his daughter. One of several Ealing essays in the supernatural.

1940   The Proud Valley

Directed by Penrose Tennyson, script by Penrose Tennyson, Jack Jones, Louis Goulding from a story by Herbert Marshall, Alfredda Brilliant. With Paul Robeson, Edward Rigby, Edward Chapman, Rachel Thomas, Simon Lack.

A black stoker gets a job in a Welsh colliery, which is closed by the owners after an accident but re-opened when the miners march on London. The original script had the miners re-opening the pit themselves, but was changed when war broke out during the filming.

1942   Find, Fix and Strike

A documentary about the training of the Fleet Air Arm. Directed by Compton Bennett, produced by Cavalcanti.

1942   The Goose Steps Out

Directed by Will Hay, Basil Dearden, script by John Dighton, Angus Macphail
from a story by Bernard Miles, Reg Groves. With Will Hay, Frank Pettingell,
Julien Mitchell, Anne Firth, Charles Hawtrey.
Will Hay as a British spy masquerading as a German professor. Peter Ustinov
appears among the Hitler Youth.

1943   Went the Day Well?

Directed by Alberto Cavalcanti, script by John Dighton, Diana Morgan, Angus Macphail from a story by Graham Greene. With Leslie Banks, Valerie Taylor, Marie Lohr, David Farrar.
German paratroops, disguised as British soldiers, occupy an English village. Cavalcanti's first film for Ealing. The music was by William Walton.

1943   The Bells Go Down

Directed by Basil Dearden, script by Roger Macdougall, Stephen Black. With Tommy Trinder, Mervyn Johns, James Mason, Beatrice Varley, Finlay Currie.

Home front heroism, as represented by the volunteer fire service during the London blitz. Basil Dearden's first solo feature, it was released in the same week as Humphrey Jennings' documentary on the fire-fighters, *Fires Were Started*.

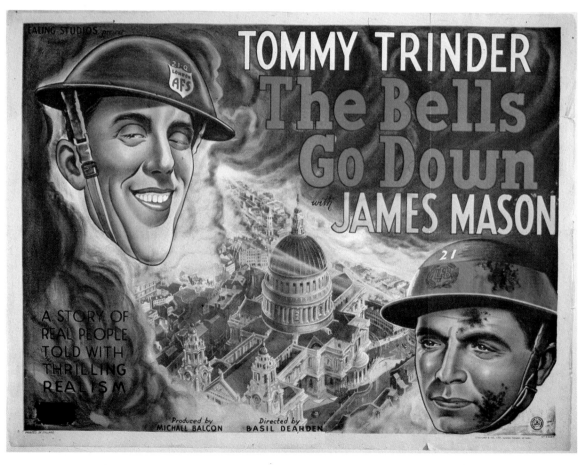

Directed by Alexander Mackendrick, script by Compton Mackenzie, Angus Macphail from the novel by Compton Mackenzie. With Basil Radford, Catherine Lacey, Wylie Watson, Joan Greenwood, Bruce Seton, James Robertson Justice, Gordon Jackson. Suffering from a wartime shortage of whisky, the inhabitants of a remote Scottish island take advantage when a freighter laden with whisky is wrecked off their coast. Alexander Mackendrick's first film as director, shot entirely on location on the Hebridean island of Barra. The American title was *Tight Little Island*.

1957 Barnacle Bill

Directed by Charles Frend, script by T.E.B. Clarke. With Alec Guinness, Maurice Denham, Irene Browne, Victor Maddern.
Alec Guinness as a seasick captain whose last command is a dilapidated seaside pier. The last of the comedies scripted by T.E.B. Clarke.

Films

Another Shore 42,43
Barnacle Bill 64
Bells Go Down, The 62
Bitter Springs 35
Black Magic 47
Blue Lamp, The 20
Cage of Gold 6
Captive Heart, The 15
Champagne Charlie 2
Chinese Cat, The 54
Cruel Sea, The 44,45
Dead of Night 28,29
Dreaming 55
Eureka Stockade 38
Find, Fix and Strike 59
For Those in Peril 1
Frieda 4
Gentle Gunman, The 21
Ghost of St. Michael's, The 23
Goose Steps Out, The 60
Halfway House, The 57
Headline 9
Hue and Cry 16,17
It Always Rains on Sunday 19
Jade Mask, The 3
Johnny Frenchman 26
Kind Hearts and Coronets 25
Ladykillers, The 41
Lavender Hill Mob, The 7
Let George Do It 33

Love Lottery, The 50,51
Loves of Joanna
    Godden, The 36,37
Magnet, The 12,13
Man in the White Suit, The 8
Nicholas Nickleby 10,11
Overlanders, The 27
Painted Boats 49
Passport to Pimlico 5
Pink String and
    Sealing Wax 48
Pool of London 22
Proud Valley, The 58
Return of the Vikings, The 52
San Demetrio London 30,31
Saraband for Dead Lovers 34
They Came to a City 53
Titfield Thunderbolt, The 18
Train of Events 40
Went the Day Well? 61
West of Zanzibar 56
Where No Vultures Fly 39
Whisky Galore! 63

Designers and artists

Ardizzone, Edward 10-12
Bainbridge, John 15
Bawden, Edward 16,18
Bentley, Nicolas 5
Boswell, James 19-22
Chapman, George 23
Fitton, James 25
Fraser, Eric 2
Freedman, Barnett 2,26
Goetz, Walter 27
Hurry, Leslie 28-9
Kestleman, Morris 30-1
Lambda, Peter 33
Medley, Robert 34-5
Minton, John 36,38-9
Mount, Reginald 40-1
Mozley, Charles 42
Murray, Charles 44
Peake, Mervyn 47
Piper, John 48-9
Robb, Brian 50
Roberts, Bruce 52
Rothholz, H.A. 53
Rowe, Clifford 54-5
Searle, Ronald 7
Thompson, A.R. 8
Walklin, Colin 45
Winslade, 56
Woods, S. John 1-9
Wright, Matvyn 57